cooking the French way

Apple slices combined with apple cider and spices make pork chops Normandy style a unique and delicious dish. (Recipe on page 32.)

cooking the French way

LYNNE MARIE WALDEE

easy menu
ethnic
cookbooks

Lerner Publications Company ■ Minneapolis

Series Editor: Patricia A. Grotts
Series Consultant: Ann L. Burckhardt

Drawings and Map by Jeanette Swofford

The page border in this book is based on the *fleur-de-lis* design that was used on the French flag from the 1300s to the 1600s. Although the word *fleur-de-lis* means "flower of the lily," the flower shown in the symbol is not a lily but an iris. Some historians believe the iris was once called a lily.

The fabrics shown in some of the drawings in this book are from Provence, a province in southern France.

ACKNOWLEDGMENTS: The illustrations are reproduced through the courtesy of: pp. 2, 4, 17, 20, 40, Robert L. Wolfe; p. 9, French Government Tourist Office; pp. 18, 48, Food and Wines from France; p. 22, American Egg Board; p. 24, General Foods; pp. 28, 42, Burch Communications, Inc.; p. 34, United Dairy Industry Association; p. 38, California Strawberry Advisory Board. Cover photograph by Robert L. Wolfe.

Library of Congress Cataloging in Publication Data

Waldee, Lynne Marie.
  Cooking the French way.

  (Easy menu ethnic cookbooks)
  Includes index.
  Summary: An introduction to the cooking of France, featuring basic recipes for everyday breakfast, lunch, and dinner dishes. Also includes typical menus and a brief description of the special features of a French table setting.
  1. Cookery, French—Juvenile literature.
2. France—Juvenile literature. [1. Cookery, French]
I. Title. II. Series.
TX719.W28   641.5944   82-258
ISBN 0-8225-0904-0   AACR2

Manufactured in the United States of America

7 8 9 10 11 – P/JR – 99 98 97 96 95

CONTENTS

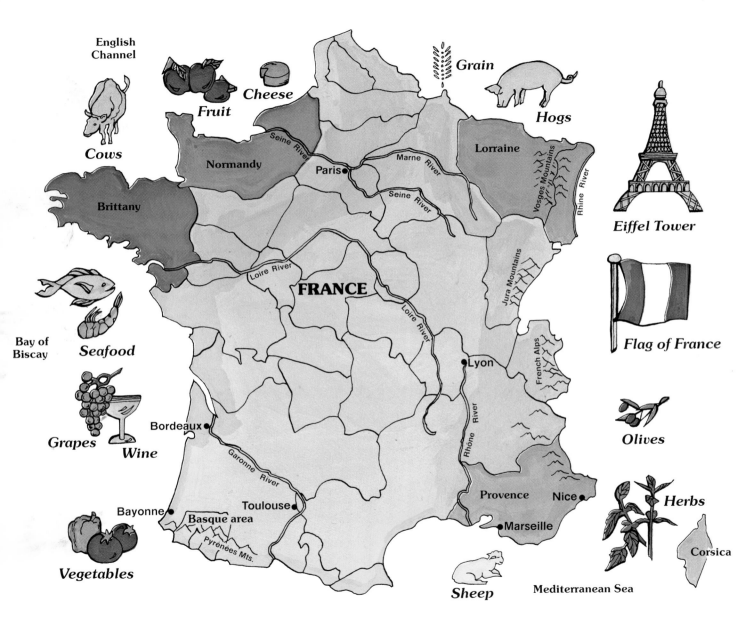

English Channel

Fruit

Cheese

Grain

Hogs

Cows

Normandy

Lorraine

Paris

Marne River

Seine River

Vosges Mountains

Rhine River

Eiffel Tower

Brittany

Loire River

FRANCE

Jura Mountains

Flag of France

Bay of Biscay

Seafood

Loire River

French Alps

Lyon

Grapes

Wine

Bordeaux

Garonne River

Rhône River

Olives

Bayonne

Toulouse

Basque area

Provence

Nice

Herbs

Pyrénées Mts.

Marseille

Corsica

Vegetables

Sheep

Mediterranean Sea

INTRODUCTION

The people of France consider cooking a fine art. Just as an artist carves out a statue hidden within a block of stone, a French cook brings out the flavor locked inside each simple vegetable and piece of meat. The French cook then arranges the food so that its shapes and colors are combined in the most attractive way possible.

A French saying describes the attitude of French cooks toward their art: *"L'exces en tout est defaut"*—excess is always a fault. In other words, you can have too much of a good thing. French cooks use strong flavors, such as garlic, in small amounts so that they will not overpower other flavors. In fact, the most important rule in French cooking is not to use too much of any one ingredient.

THE KINDS OF FRENCH COOKING

There are two distinctly different kinds of cooking in France. One kind is quite grand and the other is like home cooking. The recipes in this book are of the "home cooking" variety—delicious and easy to fix. But it is interesting to know a little about the grand type of French cooking, too. After all, once you have mastered the dishes in this book, you may want to try something more difficult!

Years ago, the chefs who worked for the kings and queens of France developed *haute* or *grande cuisine* (oht or grahn kwih-ZEEN). This kind of cooking featured huge, complicated meals that took hours of preparation and often included unusual ingredients such as rare wines and exotic fruits.

When the French nobility was overthrown in the 1789 French Revolution, the chefs who developed *haute cuisine* fled to other parts of Europe. The art of this fine cooking, however, was not lost. The French chefs spread its fame throughout Europe and even to the United States. This very special and difficult type of cooking is still practiced today by famous chefs in elegant restaurants.

The other kind of French cooking is called *cuisine bourgeois* (kwih-ZEEN boor-ZHWAH). It is the kind of home cooking you would find in a small restaurant or inn or in the home of a typical French family. Old French home recipes, which have been handed down from generation to generation, are tasty and nourishing.

THE REGIONS OF FRANCE

Geography has an important effect on the cooking of each region of France. For instance, Normandy, on the northern coast, has many fields where cattle graze and orchards grow. Its cooking features apples, cream, and cheeses. Brittany, a province on the northwest coast, has very poor land for growing things and, therefore, does not have many edible plants or grazing animals. Instead, its riches come from the ocean. Cooks in Brittany prepare fine soups and other dishes using all sorts of seafood, including lobsters, shrimp, mussels, and saltwater fish.

In some regions of France, cooking is strongly affected by the traditions of neighboring countries. The snow-covered Pyrénées Mountains in the south of France are near Spain. The cooking of that region resembles Spanish cooking. It uses tomatoes, peppers, and sausages. In southeast France, the province of Provence borders Italy. Olives, as well as many herbs, grow on Provence's gently rolling hills. In the cooking of Provence, you will find plenty of olive oil and herbs such as basil, thyme, and rosemary—ingredients also used in the cooking of northern Italy.

Cheese and fresh fruit are often used in the cooking of Normandy.

The region of Normandy on the northern coast of France is known for its green fields, cattle, and orchards.

DINING IN FRANCE

If French cooking can be called an art, then dining in France can be called a ceremony! The eating of a well-prepared meal is considered one of the important pleasures of daily life. Many dining customs that have grown through centuries are still part of the daily routine in France. At mealtime, family members gather around the table. While they eat, they talk, sharing ideas and telling stories of their day's experiences. After the meal, family members go back to their own routines, but each is left with a feeling of well-being that comes from enjoying a good meal and pleasant conversation.

The recipes in this book will show you the many pleasures of French home cooking. You can enjoy preparing and eating these meals yourself, but you may enjoy them even more if you eat them French-style—in a leisurely way with your family.

BEFORE YOU BEGIN

Cooking any dish, plain or fancy, is easier and more fun if you are familiar with its ingredients. French cooking makes use of some ingredients that you may not know. You should also be familiar with the special terms that will be used in various recipes in this book. Therefore, *before* you start cooking any of the French dishes in this book, study the following "dictionary" of special ingredients and terms very carefully. Then read through the recipe you want to try from beginning to end.

Now you are ready to shop for ingredients and to organize the cookware you will need. Once you have assembled everything, you can begin to cook. It is also very important to read *The Careful Cook* on page 44 before you start. Following these rules will make your cooking experience safe, fun, and easy.

COOKING UTENSILS

crepe pan—There are many pans available that are designed specifically for crepe-making, but almost any low-sided pan with a cooking surface 6 to 8 inches in diameter will work just as well.

spatula—A flat, thin utensil, usually metal, used to lift, toss, turn, or scoop up food

whisk—A small wire utensil used for beating food by hand

Garlic and onions are often sautéed before they are added to other ingredients in a recipe. Here sautéed garlic and onions are lifted out of the pan with a spatula.

COOKING TERMS

boil—To heat a liquid over high heat until bubbles form and rise rapidly to the surface

brown—To cook food quickly in fat over high heat so that the surface turns an even brown

grate—To cut into tiny pieces by rubbing the food against a grater; to shred

hard-cook—To cook an egg in its shell until both the yolk and white are firm

mince—To chop food into very small pieces

preheat—To allow an oven to warm up to a certain temperature before putting food in it

sauté—To fry quickly over high heat in oil or fat, stirring or turning the food to prevent burning

shred—To tear or cut into small pieces, either by hand or with a grater

simmer—To cook over low heat in liquid kept just below its boiling point. Bubbles may occasionally rise to the surface.

SPECIAL INGREDIENTS

bay leaf—The dried leaf of the bay (also called laurel) tree. It is used to season meats, poultry, soups, and stews.

chives—A member of the onion family whose thin, green stalks are chopped and used to garnish salads as well as fish, egg, cheese, potato, and other vegetable dishes

Dijon-style mustard—A commercially-prepared condiment (an ingredient used to enhance the flavor of food) made from mustard seed, white wine, vinegar, salt, and spices

garlic—An herb whose distinctive flavor is used in many dishes. Fresh garlic can usually be found in the produce department of a supermarket. Each piece or bulb can be broken up into several small sections called cloves. Most recipes use only one or two finely chopped cloves of this very strong herb. Before you chop up a clove of garlic, you will have to remove the brittle, papery covering that surrounds it.

Gruyère cheese—A hard, tangy, light yellow cheese from Switzerland

leek—An herb in the onion family, but smaller and milder in taste than an onion. The bulb of the leek is used to flavor soups and stews and is also served as a vegetable.

nutmeg—A fragrant spice, either whole or ground, that is often used in desserts

olive oil—An oil made from pressed olives that is used in cooking and for dressing salads

Parmesan cheese—A very hard, sharply flavored, yellow Italian cheese that is usually grated for use in cooking and also used as a garnish for soups and salads

red wine vinegar—A vinegar made with red wine that is often used with oil for dressing salads

thyme—The leaves of a bushy shrub that grows mainly in California and France. It is used as an herb in cooking and has a very strong flavor.

A FRENCH TABLE

Simplicity is the key to decorating the table in most French homes. Because the appearance, smell, and taste of carefully prepared foods are the central concerns of the French cook, decorations and extra dishes on the table are kept to a minimum. Simple place settings and cloth napkins (never paper) are used on plain or checked cloths.

Fragrant flowers are never used on the table because their scent could detract from the aroma of the food and, therefore, the enjoyment of the meal. But a small collection of condiments is usually found on the table. These often include oil and vinegar in cruets (glass bottles), wine-based French mustard in a bowl with a small wooden spoon, salt, and peppercorns in a pepper mill. Such seasonings add sparkle to the meal, and their containers decorate the table.

A FRENCH MENU

Below is a simplified menu plan for a typical day of French cooking. The French names of the dishes are given, along with a guide on how to pronounce them. Three alternate lunch and two dinner ideas are included. Recipes for the starred items can be found in this book.

ENGLISH	FRANÇAIS	PRONUNCIATION GUIDE
MENU	LA CARTE	*lah kart*
Breakfast	**Le Petit Déjeuner**	luh puh-TEE day-zhuh-NAY
French pastries	Croissant, Baguette	kwah-SAHN, bah-GET
*Hot chocolate	Chocolat	shoh-koh-LAH
Lunch	**Le Déjeuner**	luh day-zhuh-NAY
I	I	
*Potato-and-leek soup or *Quiche Lorraine	Potage parmentier ou Quiche Lorraine	poh-TAHZH par-mehn-TYAY oo keesh lor-ANE
Bread	Pain	pahn
*Green salad	Salade verte	sah-LAHD vehrt
*Vinaigrette dressing	Vinaigrette	vihn-eh-GREHT
II	II	
*Salade Niçoise	Salade Niçoise	sah-LAHD nee-SWAHZ
Bread	Pain	pahn
III	III	
*Ham and broccoli crepes with *Mornay sauce	Crêpes au broccoli et jambon avec sauce Mornay	krep oh brah-coh-LEE ay zhahm-BON ah-VEK sahs mor-NAY
Bread	Pain	pahn

ENGLISH	FRANÇAIS	PRONUNCIATION GUIDE
Snack	**Le Casse-Croûte**	luh kahs-KROOT
*Chocolate pastry	Brioche au chocolat	bree-OSH oh shoh-koh-LAH
*Croque Monsieur	Croque Monsieur	krohk meh-SYEUR
Milk or coffee	Lait ou café	lay oo kah-FAY
Dinner	**Le Dîner**	luh DEE-nay
I	I	
Clear soup	Bouillon	bwee-YOHN
*Pork chops Normandy style	Côtelettes de porc Normande	kote-LET duh por nor-MAHND
*Potato cake	Galette de pommes de terre	gah-LET duh pum duh tehr
*Green peas French style	Petits pois à la Française	puh-TEE pwah ah lah frahn-SEZ
*Green salad	Salade verte	sah-LAHD vehrt
Bread	Pain	pahn
*Crepes with Strawberries	Crêpes aux fraises	krep oh frehz
II	II	
Appetizer	Hors d'oeuvre	or deuve
*Sautéed chicken	Sauté de poulet	soh-TAY duh poo-LAY
Boiled potatoes	Pommes de terre bouillé	pum duh tehr bwee-YAY
*Glazed carrots	Carottes Vichy	kare-AWT vee-SHEE
*Green salad	Salade verte	sah-LAHD vehrt
*Pears Helen or	Poires Hélène ou	pwahr ay-LEN oo
*Chocolate mousse	Mousse au chocolat	moos oh shoh-koh-LAH

BREAKFAST/
Le Petit Déjeuner

Climate often shapes eating habits. In cold countries, many people eat hearty breakfasts of hot cereal, eggs, bacon, and fried potatoes. But in France, which has a fairly mild climate, breakfast is generally very light. A typical French breakfast might include a pastry and strong coffee or hot chocolate.

The pastries that the French enjoy in the morning are the *croissant,* a flaky, crescent-shaped roll, and the *baguette,* a long, thin, crisp French bread. These morning treats are eaten with unsalted butter and jam. Since *croissants* and *baguettes* are hard to make at home, most French people buy these and other pastries and breads daily at a bakery. *Café au lait* (kah-FAY oh lay), a strong coffee mixed with hot, foamy milk, or *chocolat,* the French version of American hot chocolate, completes the morning meal.

Chocolate first came to France from Spain through the port of Bayonne. This is a city on France's western coast in the Basque area bordering Spain. Chocolate was originally brought to Spain in 1528 by Hernando Cortés, the conqueror of Mexico.

Hot Chocolate/
Chocolat

**2 ounces sweet chocolate, broken
   into bits, or milk-chocolate chips
2 tablespoons water
2 cups milk**

1. Place chocolate and water in a small, heavy-bottomed saucepan over very low heat. Cover the pan and let chocolate soften until it is just melted.
2. Remove the saucepan from the heat and beat chocolate into a smooth paste.
3. In a different saucepan, heat milk until it boils.
4. Add 6 tablespoons of milk to chocolate paste to dilute it. Then add remaining milk, stirring constantly.
5. Pour into mugs.

Serves 2

Hot chocolate and golden croissants are often served for breakfast in France.

Crusty French bread is served at practically every meal, and cheese is also often found on French tables. As a light dessert, it is eaten alone or with fresh fruit.

LUNCH/
Le Déjeuner

In the countryside and small towns of France, the main meal is served around noon. The small meal is usually served in the evening, between 7 and 8 P.M. People who live in the large cities of France often have their small meal in the middle of the day, as most North Americans do. The recipes given here will make a delicious noon lunch, or you can eat them for a light evening meal.

Hearty soups are often served as the main course of a French luncheon. The soup is always accompanied by crusty French bread, which may be used to soak up the last drops of broth. The practice of mopping up a soup or sauce with bread is *not* considered bad manners in France. In fact, it is done at almost every meal at which a delicious soup or sauce is served.

Eggs are rarely served for breakfast in France but are often used in luncheon or dinner dishes such as omelets, soufflés, and quiches. Salads are usually served between the main course and dessert. A light dessert of cheese and fruit completes a typical French luncheon. A good combination is *Brie* (bree) cheese and crisp, tart apples.

Soup, French bread, cheese, and fruit make a typical French lunch.

Serve potato-and-leek soup and French bread for a nutritious and economical lunch.

Potato-and-Leek Soup/
Potage Parmentier

This creamy soup, along with French bread, makes a delicious and filling meal. Leftover soup keeps well in the refrigerator and can be reheated the next day. (Make sure that you don't boil the soup because boiling will make the cream curdle or form lumps.) This soup can also be eaten cold. The French then call it vichyssoise *(vish-ee-SWAHZ).*

3 medium-sized potatoes, peeled and sliced 1/8 inch thick
3 medium-sized leeks, washed thoroughly and sliced 1/8 inch thick (do not use the tough, dark green part), or 3 medium-sized yellow onions, thinly sliced
3 10¾-ounce cans (about 4½ cups) chicken broth
1 chicken broth can of cold water
½ cup whipping cream (add up to an extra ½ cup milk if you like your soup thin)
2 tablespoons butter or margarine

2 teaspoons salt
¼ teaspoon pepper
chopped chives

1. Combine potatoes, leeks or onions, chicken broth, and water in a large heavy pot or saucepan and cover.
2. Bring to a boil over medium-high heat. Reduce heat and simmer 35 to 45 minutes or until vegetables are tender.
3. Without draining off broth, mash vegetables in the saucepan with a vegetable (potato) masher until they are fairly smooth. (If they will not mash easily, soup has not cooked long enough. Let it simmer 10 to 15 minutes longer.)
4. Add cream, butter, salt, and pepper and heat soup just to the boiling point. *(Do not boil.)*
5. Sprinkle each serving with chives.

Serves 4 or 5

Although the French do not usually eat eggs for breakfast, *quiche Lorraine* is frequently served for Sunday brunch.

Quiche Lorraine

Quiche Lorraine, *a main-dish pie, is made of cream, eggs, and bacon. Many cooks add cheese to these ingredients. This specialty takes its name from the area in France called Lorraine, which is famous for its bacon.*

4 eggs
1 cup whipping cream
¼ teaspoon salt
dash of pepper
¼ teaspoon nutmeg
1 9-inch deep-dish unbaked pie shell (shell can be bought frozen in a store)
4 to 6 ounces Swiss cheese, thinly sliced or grated (1 to 1½ cups when grated)
8 ounces bacon, lightly browned and crumbled

1. Preheat the oven to 350°.
2. In a medium-sized mixing bowl, beat eggs, cream, salt, pepper, and nutmeg with an eggbeater or a whisk.
3. With a fork, prick sides and bottom of unbaked pie shell about every half inch. (This will keep pie shell from shrinking or bubbling while it is baking.)
4. Make 2 or 3 layers of cheese and bacon bits in bottom of pie shell. Pour egg-and-cream mixture over this.
5. Bake 45 to 50 minutes or until quiche is golden brown and puffy.
6. Let cool a few minutes and slice into serving pieces. Refrigerate leftovers and reheat or eat cold the next day.

Serves 4 or 5

Salade Niçoise, a colorful main or side dish, can be made with or without tuna.

Salade Niçoise

This vegetable salad is a hearty main meal by itself. If you want to serve it as just one course of a meal, leave out the tuna fish. You can also vary the other ingredients in this recipe. Try adding carrots, celery, peas, slices of hard-cooked eggs, or slivered almonds. Experiment and enjoy!

1 small head of lettuce
6 medium-sized cold cooked
      potatoes, sliced, or 1-pound can
      small whole white potatoes
½ pound fresh green beans or
      1 10-ounce package frozen green
      beans, cooked, cold, and cut into
      ½-inch lengths
6 tomatoes, quartered
½ cup vinaigrette dressing (see page
      26)
1 13-ounce can tuna, drained (optional)
      black or green olives for garnish
      (optional)

1. Wash and separate lettuce leaves, throwing away any that are wilted or discolored. Arrange leaves decoratively in a large, shallow serving plate and set aside.
2. In a large mixing bowl, combine potatoes, beans, and tomatoes. Pour vinaigrette dressing over vegetables. Using 2 spoons, carefully toss vegetables until they are thoroughly coated.
3. Spoon vegetables onto lettuce leaves and top with mound of tuna and/or olives. (Or, if you prefer, arrange vegetables and tuna as shown in the photo.)
4. Serve at once.

Serves 4 or 5

Green Salad/
Salade Verte

Green salads are served after the main dish "to clear the palate." This means that the lettuce and light dressing refresh your taste buds, preparing them for the new flavors of dessert.

1 small head of Boston lettuce
1 small head of romaine or 1 medium-sized head of iceberg lettuce
3 tablespoons chopped fresh parsley

1. To prepare salad greens, wash Boston lettuce and romaine thoroughly. Separate leaves, throwing away any that are wilted or discolored. Drain by placing leaves on paper towels. Place clean greens in a plastic bag along with the paper towels, which will absorb any remaining water. Refrigerate for at least half an hour.
2. Before serving, tear greens into bite-sized pieces and place them in a large salad bowl. Sprinkle with parsley.
3. Pour about half of vinaigrette dressing over greens. Toss with a fork and spoon until greens are well coated and no dressing remains in bottom of bowl.

Serves 4 or 5

Vinaigrette Dressing/
Vinaigrette

1 clove garlic
1 teaspoon salt
3 tablespoons red wine vinegar
¼ teaspoon pepper
6 tablespoons olive or vegetable oil

1. Chop garlic into very fine pieces and put in a small bowl.
2. Use the back of a spoon to mash garlic. Then mix it with salt.
3. Add vinegar and pepper, stirring until smooth.
4. Place in a small jar with a tight-fitting lid. Add oil, screw on lid, and shake until well blended.

Enough for 4 or 5 salad servings

Basic Crepe Batter

These delicate pancakes made of egg and flour batter are both fun to make and delicious. They are often filled with meat, fish, or vegetables, covered with a sauce, and served as a main course. Dessert crepes are made with a sweeter batter and are often filled with fruit (see page 39).

4 eggs
¼ teaspoon salt
2 cups all-purpose flour

2¼ cups milk
¼ cup melted butter

1. Combine eggs and salt in a bowl.
2. Alternately stir in flour and milk. Then beat with a whisk or electric mixer until creamy.
3. Beat in melted butter.
4. Chill batter at least 1 hour.
5. Cook in a crepe pan as shown in the illustration.

Makes 32 to 36 crepes

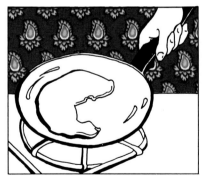

1. Lightly grease your pan if it doesn't have a non-stick surface. Then heat the pan for several seconds, lift it above the stove, and pour in 2 or 3 tablespoons of batter. 2. Quickly swirl the batter around the pan so that a thin, even layer covers the bottom. Set the pan back on the burner and cook the crepe over medium heat. 3. When the crepe bottom is brown, carefully flip the crepe over with a spatula. The other side of the crepe will brown in a few seconds. Then remove the crepe from the pan with a spatula.

Garnish ham and broccoli crepes with shredded cheese and broccoli florets.

Ham and Broccoli Crepes with Mornay Sauce/
Crêpes au Broccoli et Jambon avec Sauce Mornay

**1 pound fresh broccoli spears or
   2 8-ounce packages frozen
   broccoli spears
12 basic crepes
12 thin slices boiled ham
   Mornay sauce**

1. Cook broccoli spears in lightly salted water until tender (about 10 to 15 minutes). Slice each spear in half.
2. Preheat the oven to 400°.
3. Spread out crepes and cover each crepe with a slice of ham.
4. Place 2 or 3 broccoli spears on top of ham and roll up crepes.
5. Place crepes in a buttered ovenproof dish. Dot surface of crepes with butter and bake at 400° for 15 minutes.
6. Cover with Mornay sauce and serve.

Makes 12 crepes

Mornay Sauce/
Sauce Mornay

**1 tablespoon butter
1 tablespoon all-purpose flour
1 cup milk
3 tablespoons grated Swiss cheese
1 tablespoon grated Parmesan cheese
½ teaspoon mild prepared mustard
   (Dijon-style is best)
   salt and pepper**

1. Melt butter in a saucepan.
2. Remove from heat and stir in flour with a whisk.
3. Return to medium heat. Add milk slowly, stirring constantly until sauce is thickened.
4. Add remaining ingredients, salt and pepper to taste, and serve.

Makes about 1¼ cups

SNACK/
Le Casse-Croûte

The custom in France is to have a mid-afternoon snack of very strong coffee and a pastry or bread. *Brioches* are yeast breads rich in eggs and butter. They make delicious snacks and are generally eaten warm with unsalted butter and jam.

Since *brioches* are difficult to prepare at home, many French families buy these treats when they buy their day's supply of bread from one of the many excellent bakeries that can be found all over France. Perhaps you live near a bakery that sells French breads and pastries.

The following recipe will make a snack that is something like the French *brioche*. If you are not able to shop at a French bakery, you can bake this very special treat.

Chocolate Pastry/
Brioche au Chocolat

1 package refrigerated crescent rolls
6 tablespoons semisweet chocolate chips
 powdered sugar (enough to sprinkle lightly on each pastry)

1. Preheat the oven to 400°.
2. Remove dough according to directions on package. Smooth out perforations (dotted lines) in dough with your fingers and cut dough into 6 rectangles.
3. In the center of each rectangle, place 1 tablespoon of chocolate chips. Bring each of the 4 corners of the rectangle to the middle and seal to make an envelope.
4. Place pastries on an ungreased cookie sheet and bake 10 to 15 minutes or until golden.
5. Remove and place pastries on a cooling rack. Sprinkle tops lightly with powdered sugar.
6. Serve while pastries are slightly warm.
Makes 6

Croque Monsieur

A delicious hot snack

2 thick slices cooked ham
4 thick slices white bread, with crusts
**   cut off**
4 ounces Swiss or Gruyère cheese,
**   grated (1 cup when grated)**
3 tablespoons butter
2 teaspoons all-purpose flour
1 cup milk, heated
**   pepper**
1 egg

1. Put ham slice on each of 2 bread slices. Then press all but 2 tablespoons grated cheese on top of ham.
2. Make sandwiches by firmly pressing another bread slice on top of each.
3. Heat 1 tablespoon butter, stir in flour, and let cook 1 minute.
4. Add warm milk and stir until thick and creamy.
5. Add 2 remaining tablespoons grated cheese. Add pepper to taste. Keep this sauce warm, but do not boil.

6. Beat egg and dip 2 sandwiches in it, making sure both sides of each sandwich are soaked.
7. Fry sandwiches in 2 remaining tablespoons butter until golden and crisp on both sides.
8. Pour cheese sauce over each sandwich and serve.

Serves 2

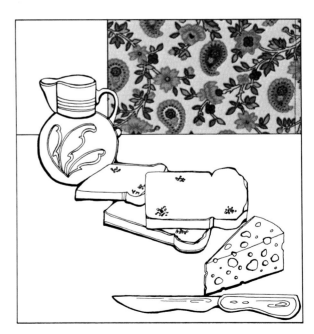

DINNER/
Le Dîner

The main meal of the day can be quite an event in France. If guests dine with the family, there may be four or five courses, each brought to the table separately, and special wines are chosen to go with the foods being served.

Fancy dinners with many courses may last for several hours. When the dishes are finally cleared away, the diners top off their evening of tasty food and lively conversation with cups of strong black coffee.

At quiet dinners when the family dines alone, plain but delicious home cooking is in order. There are fewer courses, and only ordinary table wine is served. But the tradition of good food and talk is still carried on, for dinner is the one time during the day when the members of the family can be together.

Pork Chops
Normandy Style/
Côtelettes de Porc
Normande

2 tablespoons butter or margarine
1 tablespoon olive or vegetable oil
4 pork chops, about 1 inch thick
1 clove garlic, minced
1 medium-sized onion, thinly sliced
1¼ cups apple cider
¼ teaspoon nutmeg
1½ teaspoons salt
   dash of pepper
1 large tart apple, peeled, cored, and
   cut into ¼-inch-thick slices
2 tablespoons brown sugar
3 tablespoons whipping cream

1. Heat butter and oil in a large skillet. Add chops and brown over medium-high heat. Reduce heat slightly and cook chops 6 minutes on each side.
2. Remove chops from the skillet and place on a serving platter. Pour off all but about 3 tablespoons fat from the skillet.

3. Put garlic and onion in the skillet and sauté until onions are tender but not browned (about 5 minutes).

4. Add apple cider. Simmer sauce, covered, for 5 minutes.

5. Return pork chops to the skillet. Sprinkle with nutmeg, salt, and pepper. Arrange apple slices over pork chops and sprinkle chops and apples with brown sugar.

6. Cover and simmer for 15 to 20 minutes or until chops and apples are tender.

7. Stir cream into the skillet with a whisk. Simmer 5 minutes, uncovered.

8. Spoon apple slices and sauce over pork chops as you serve them.

Serves 4

Fresh watercress and rosemary add the finishing touch to delicious sautéed chicken.

Sautéed Chicken/
Sauté de Poulet

**1 2½- to 3-pound chicken, cut into
    serving pieces**
**⅓ cup all-purpose flour combined with
    ½ teaspoon salt, ¼ teaspoon
    thyme, and ¼ teaspoon pepper**
2 tablespoons butter or margarine
1 tablespoon olive or vegetable oil
½ teaspoon thyme
1 bay leaf, finely crumbled
2 cloves garlic, finely chopped
1½ cups canned chicken broth
**1 3-ounce can sliced mushrooms,
    drained (optional)**

1. Wash chicken pieces under cool
running water. Pat dry with paper towels.
2. Put seasoned flour in a small,
clean brown paper bag. Place chicken
pieces in the bag, one at a time, and
shake to coat with flour.
3. Heat butter and oil in a large skillet
or heavy pot. Add chicken and brown on
both sides over medium-high heat.
Reduce heat to low and cook, covered,
for 20 minutes, turning chicken twice.
4. Sprinkle chicken pieces with thyme,
bay leaf, and garlic. Slowly pour chicken
broth and mushrooms into the skillet.
5. Stir gently. Cover the skillet, but leave
a small opening that steam can escape
through. Cook over low heat for about
30 minutes or until about half of the sauce
has cooked away and chicken is tender.
6. Spoon sauce over chicken pieces as
you serve them.

Serves 4

Potato Cake/
Galette de Pommes de Terre

Buttery potato cake is a delicious side dish that goes well with any kind of meat or fish.

6 medium-sized baking potatoes, thinly sliced
salt and pepper to taste
⅓ cup melted butter or margarine

1. Place a layer of potato slices in the bottom of a greased 9-inch pie plate.
2. Season with small amount of salt and pepper. Repeat until all potato slices have been used.
3. Pour butter evenly over potatoes.
4. Do not cover dish. Cook in a 400° oven until potatoes are tender (about 50 minutes).
5. Gently loosen the sides and bottom of cake with a spatula. Flip over onto a serving plate. Cut into wedges to serve.

Serves 6

Green Peas French Style/
Petits Pois à la Française

2 pounds fresh peas or 1 10-ounce
   package frozen tiny green peas
1 teaspoon sugar
½ teaspoon salt
   dash of pepper
2 tablespoons minced fresh parsley
1½ cups finely shredded lettuce
¼ cup butter or margarine
1 tablespoon water

1. If you have fresh peas, shell just before using.
2. Place all ingredients in a medium-sized saucepan and stir gently.
3. Cover tightly and cook over low heat for 20 minutes or until peas are tender. (For frozen peas, cover tightly and cook over low heat for 8 minutes. Then stir with a fork to break up any remaining frozen peas. Replace cover and cook 3 to 7 minutes longer or until peas are tender.)

Serves 4

Glazed Carrots/
Carottes Vichy

1 pound carrots, peeled and thinly
   sliced
¼ cup water
   dash of salt
3 tablespoons butter or margarine
1 teaspoon sugar

1. Place all ingredients in a medium-sized saucepan, stir, and cover tightly. Cook over low heat for about 10 minutes or until carrots are tender and glazed (covered evenly with the thick liquid), and most of remaining liquid has cooked away.
2. Stir to coat with remaining liquid and serve.

Serves 4

To make strawberry crepes even more attractive, arrange them so the fruit is showing at the ends of each.

Dessert Crepe Batter

4 eggs
1 cup all-purpose flour
2 tablespoons sugar
1 cup milk
¼ cup water
1 tablespoon melted butter

1. Beat eggs in a bowl.
2. Slowly add flour and sugar alternately with milk and water. Then beat with a whisk or electric mixer until smooth.
3. Beat in melted butter.
4. Chill batter at least 1 hour.
5. Cook in a crepe pan as shown in the illustration on page 27.

Makes 20 to 25 crepes

Crepes with Strawberries/ Crêpes aux Fraises

These crepes can easily be filled with other kinds of fresh fruit. Try using 3 cups of blueberries or sliced peaches instead of the strawberries. Delicious!

3 cups fresh sliced strawberries
⅓ cup granulated sugar
8 ounces (1 cup) cottage cheese
8 ounces (1 cup) sour cream
½ cup powdered sugar
10 to 12 dessert crepes

1. Combine strawberries and granulated sugar. Set aside.
2. Beat cottage cheese in a blender or with an electric mixer until smooth. Add sour cream and powdered sugar and stir well.
3. Use about ⅔ of fruit and creamy mixture to fill crepes. Fold crepes over.
4. Top with remaining fruit and creamy mixture or top with fruit and powdered sugar.

Makes 10 to 12 crepes

The flavors of chocolate, raspberry, and vanilla are combined with pear halves to create pears Helen. Serve this dessert in clear glass dishes to show off its colorful layers.

Pears Helen/
Poires Hélène

½ cup chocolate syrup
4 to 8 scoops vanilla ice cream
4 canned pear halves, drained
⅓ cup raspberry or strawberry jam
1 tablespoon hot water

1. In the bottom of each of 4 sherbet glasses or bowls, put 2 tablespoons chocolate syrup.
2. On top of syrup, place 1 or 2 scoops of ice cream.
3. Place pear half, cut side down, on top of each portion of ice cream.
4. Combine jam and water in a separate bowl and spoon mixture over each pear.

Serves 4

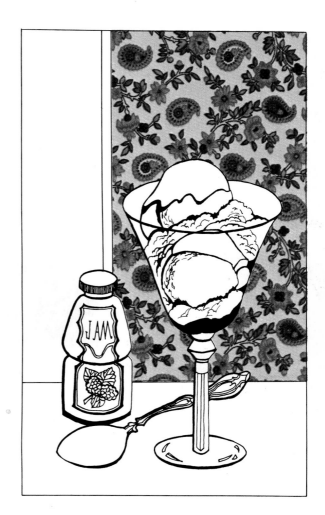

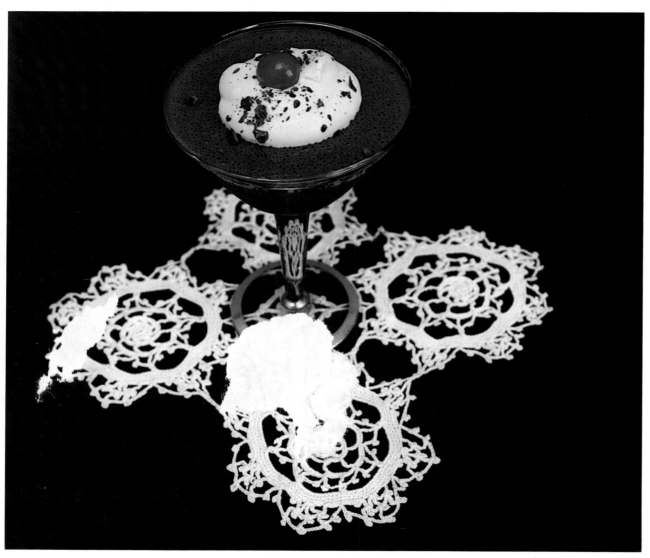

Rich chocolate mousse is an easy yet mouth-watering dessert that your family and friends will love.

Chocolate Mousse/
Mousse au Chocolat

Chocolate mousse is often made with unsweetened chocolate and has a bitter, strong flavor. This recipe, however, is for a light, sweet-tasting mousse that is sure to appeal to all chocolate-lovers.

1 **egg**
1 **egg yolk**
1 **6-ounce package semisweet**
   chocolate chips
1 **teaspoon vanilla extract**
1 **cup milk, heated**
   pinch of salt

1. Blend all ingredients in a blender for 1 minute at medium speed. (An electric mixer can be used, but chocolate chips should be melted first.)
2. Pour into dessert glasses. Chill several hours or overnight before serving.

Serves 4

THE CAREFUL COOK

Whenever you cook, there are certain safety rules you must always keep in mind. Even experienced cooks follow these rules when they are in the kitchen.

1. Always wash your hands before handling food.
2. Thoroughly wash all raw vegetables and fruits to remove dirt, chemicals, and insecticides.
3. Use a cutting board when cutting up vegetables and fruits. Don't cut them up in your hand! And be sure to cut in a direction *away* from you and your fingers.
4. Long hair or loose clothing can easily catch fire if brought near the burners of a stove. If you have long hair, tie it back before you start cooking.
5. Turn all pot handles toward the back of the stove so that you will not catch your sleeves or jewelry on them. This is especially important when younger brothers and sisters are around. They could easily knock off a pot and get burned.

6. Always use a pot holder to steady hot pots or to take pans out of the oven. Don't use a wet cloth on a hot pan because the steam it produces could burn you.
7. Lift the lid of a steaming pot with the opening away from you so that you will not get burned.
8. If you get burned, hold the burn under cold running water. Do not put grease or butter on it. Cold water helps to take the heat out, but grease or butter will only keep it in.
9. If grease or cooking oil catches fire, throw baking soda or salt at the bottom of the flame to put it out. (Water will *not* put out a grease fire.) Call for help, and try to turn all the stove burners to "off."

METRIC CONVERSION CHART

WHEN YOU KNOW		MULTIPLY BY	TO FIND	
MASS (weight)				
ounces	(oz)	28.0	grams	(g)
pounds	(lb)	0.45	kilograms	(kg)
VOLUME				
teaspoons	(tsp)	5.0	milliliters	(ml)
tablespoons	(Tbsp)	15.0	milliliters	
fluid ounces	(oz)	30.0	milliliters	
cup	(c)	0.24	liters	(l)
pint	(pt)	0.47	liters	
quart	(qt)	0.95	liters	
gallon	(gal)	3.8	liters	
TEMPERATURE				
Fahrenheit	(°F)	5/9 (after	Celsius	(°C)
temperature		subtracting 32)	temperature	

COMMON MEASURES AND THEIR EQUIVALENTS

3 teaspoons = 1 tablespoon

8 tablespoons = ½ cup

2 cups = 1 pint

2 pints = 1 quart

4 quarts = 1 gallon

16 ounces = 1 pound

INDEX

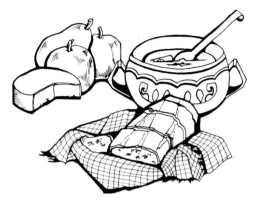

ABOUT THE AUTHOR

Lynne Marie Waldee, a native of St. Charles, Minnesota, graduated from St. Olaf College in Northfield, Minnesota, with a degree in political science. Later she graduated from Vanderbilt University Law School in Tennessee. She currently lives in New York City and works as a municipal bond lawyer on Wall Street.

Waldee has loved to cook ever since the second grade, when her mother taught her how to make gingerbread cookies. She has traveled widely in France and has studied classical French cooking with instructor Peter Kump in New York City. In addition to French cooking, Waldee enjoys reading, traveling, and collecting antiques.

easy menu ethnic cookbooks

Cooking the **AFRICAN** Way
Cooking the **AUSTRALIAN** Way
Cooking the **AUSTRIAN** Way
Cooking the **CARIBBEAN** Way
Cooking the **CHINESE** Way
Cooking the **ENGLISH** Way
Cooking the **FRENCH** Way
Cooking the **GERMAN** Way
Cooking the **GREEK** Way
Cooking the **HUNGARIAN** Way
Cooking the **INDIAN** Way
Cooking the **ISRAELI** Way
Cooking the **ITALIAN** Way
Cooking the **JAPANESE** Way
Cooking the **KOREAN** Way
Cooking the **LEBANESE** Way
Cooking the **MEXICAN** Way
Cooking the **NORWEGIAN** Way
Cooking the **POLISH** Way
Cooking the **RUSSIAN** Way
Cooking the **SOUTH AMERICAN** Way
Cooking the **SPANISH** Way
Cooking the **SWISS** Way
Cooking the **THAI** Way
Cooking the **VIETNAMESE** Way

DESSERTS Around the World
Ethnic Cooking the **MICROWAVE** Way
HOLIDAY Cooking Around the World
How to Cook a **GOOSEBERRY FOOL**
VEGETARIAN Cooking Around the World